Girlz Inc.

Workbook & Guide To Success

By: Bianda Shana Taylor

Quote

"If girls can write what they feel, beauty can be on the inside."

Bianda Taylor

Dedication

Girlz Inc. Is dedicated to every single girl in the world who aspires to dream and be more than who they see in the mirror. You were created to live, create, hope, and achieve greatness. Be someone of good character and humility. Let your kindness shine through any place that's dark. Never be afraid to do what's right.

Love, Bianda

Acknowledgements

I would like to acknowledge North side Community Center of St. Louis Mo. Attending North side Community Center gave me the momentum to dream and hope for more in this life. Thank you so much with all my heart. Thank You to Velda City Community Center for allowing me to be a Cheerleading coach at the age of 18. Leading the youth at an early stage in my life inspired me to be there for a girl every day. To my daughter Amyre and Bianda you can do anything in this life if you believe you can. To all of the girls in my family, be inspired to shoot for the stars.

Love, Bianda

Girlz Inc.

Workbook & Guide to Success

Communication

Communication- The act of transferring information from one place to another.

Communication can be used vocally, written, and using printed media. Other ways we communicate consist of books, magazines, websites, emails, visual, body language, gestures, & tone of pitch in voice.

Brain Power

Describe two other ways that communication can be used in our everyday lives.

_____

_____

_____

_____

_____

_____

Communication skills can help all aspects of life from professional or social. It is always good to practice communicating clearly and accurately.
Make a list of four ways that we can communicate positively in society.

_____

_____

_____

_____

_____

_____

_____

_____

Make a list of four ways we can communicate negatively in society.

_____

_____

_____

_____

_____

_____

_____

_____

(True or false) It is positive communication to yell at someone for accidently stepping on your shoe.

Wrap It Up

In a group create a small skit displaying positive communication. Every group member should play apart in creating the scene. Your scene will be no more than 10 minutes to play out. Have fun!

Interpersonal Communication

Interpersonal communication- Are the skills we use when engaged in face to face communication with one or several people involved.

What we say is an important way of getting our message across. We often communicate with using non-verbal signals, gestures, facial expressions, body language and appearance. We always say something whether we speak it verbally or not. People can make assumptions from what looks can be on our faces or how we are dressed.

Brain Power

Describe two ways we use interpersonal skills in society.

_____

_____

_____

_____

_____

_____

What can be two positive outcomes of using good interpersonal skills?

_____
_____
_____
_____
_____
_____

When we apply for a job it is always good interpersonal skills to make pleasant facial expressions and communicate with professional language. Doing these things can better your chance of getting the job.

What can be two negative outcome of using poor interpersonal skills?

_____
_____
_____
_____
_____
_____

(True or False) Showing up for a job interview with your favorite jeans and tee shirt well more than likely get you the job.

Wrap It Up

In a group create a scene going to a job interview. The scene should be displaying good interpersonal skills. Every group member should participate. Have fun!

Writing Skills

Writing skills- The ability to write clearly and effective.

Good writing skills can enhance the quality of letters, essays, applications, and personal documents. When we effectively use the correct way to write, it makes communication easier to understand on paper. Punctuation, spelling and grammar is very important when conveying messages.

Brain Power

Describe a time where you wrote something and someone misunderstood what you meant because of grammar or spelling.

_____

_____

_____

_____

_____

_____

_____

Correct the sentence below.

may i hav a glaz of milk pleez,

_____

_____

_____

Texting is one of the effective ways we communicate to send messages through our cell phones to the people we know. We sometimes use the wrong way of spelling a word to make it short and simple.

Have using incorrect spellings to respond in your text messages ever affected you when it was time to use it the correct way? For example on a writing assignment at school or writing a letter and you noticed you spelled it wrong the way you usually write it through texting. Share a time that you have.

_____

_____

_____

_____

_____

_____

_____

(True or false) Using the word their will describe if you are going to a place.

Wrap It Up

In a group write three correct ways to use the words their ,there, and they're. These words sound the same. They are spelled and should be used differently. A member of the group will explain in detail about why the word should be spelled that way in the sentence. Have fun!

Bullying

Bully- A person who uses strength to intimidate those who are weaker.

- Signs of bullying consist of using hurtful or threatening mean words.
- Name Calling.
- Mean looks of Intimidation.
- Asking for money with no intention of repaying.
- Hitting
- Taking things because the person won't ask for them back.
- Cruel name calling over the internet.

Brain Power

Describe two ways of bullying below that you did not see listed above.

_____

_____

_____

_____

_____

Describe a way bullying can have an effect on a person.

_____

_____

_____

_____

_____

Bullying someone is never ok. It is very damaging to someone's self esteem. Always tell a person of trust if you know of one who's being bullied. You could be the person that will help them out of a ruff situation.

People never should be bullied at any time for race, gender, personality etc. List two ways someone might be bullied.

_____

_____

_____

_____

_____

_____

(True or false) All bullies are bad people they deserve to go to jail.

Wrap It Up

In a group put together a list of 5 tips you would say to help a person speak out if they encounter a bully. Every group member's participation is needed. Have fun!

Hygiene & Wellness

Conditions are practices to maintaining health and cleanliness.

 Hygiene and wellness consist of caring about yourself physically. We have to care about the way we look & smell. Practicing smelling great and looking our best brings out beauty from the inside out.

- Bathing or showering daily
- Brushing teeth
- Wearing deodorant
- Washing your face
- Grooming your hair
- Wearing fresh washed clothes
- Pressed and wrinkle free clothing

What are two ways that we can remind ourselves to shower and bathe?

_____

_____

_____

_____

_____

_____

How can not brushing your teeth affect your smile?

_____

_____

_____

_____

_____

_____

When we take care of ourselves, looking our best we feel great and have good self-esteem. When you have an unhealthy smile, and smelly body odors people notice! They may not say anything to you but most time they will not want to be around you. Not practicing hygiene affects others around you as well. Staying sanitary when monthly cycles arrive is very important as well. Changing sanitary napkins and disposing properly can be embarrassing if not carefully managed. Having x-tra undergarments are pants to take with you in case of emergency can help at the right time. Never rely on others to have a plan for your monthly cycle. Always be prepared having one available in a private place with you at all times.

What are two conclusions people can make about you if you are not well- groomed and have poor hygiene?

_____

_____

_____

_____

_____

_____

(True or False) Having bad breath is common no one really pays attention if your breath smells.

Wrap It Up

In a group put together a skit of how someone can draw a false conclusion if you smell bad and didn't brush your teeth. Every group member should participate. Have fun!

Peer Pressure

Peer Pressure-The social influence of a group or person who persuade you to do wrong things.

Peer pressure is one of the hardest things to encounter as a young adult. Knowing how to say no and stick with it can be scary. You will always face some type of peer pressure, self confidence & Speaking out can detour a person thats trying to persuade you to do something wrong fast. Sometimes you can ask for guidance on what to about a challenge you may be facing from someone who you can trust will give you good help and advice. Never be afraid to call your parent or police if you are ever in a dangerous situation.

Brain Power

Describe two peer pressures that is the hardest for you to deal with in school.

_____

_____

_____

_____

_____

_____

What can be two things you can say to a person that is peer pressuring you?

_____

_____

_____

_____

_____

_____

Things you can say to stay strong in peer pressuring.

- Are you kidding me that's bad for my health!
- I'm not comfortable with doing that!
- I can get alcohol poisoning!
- My parents won't allow it!
- I'm okay if you don't like my choice it's for me not you!

What can be the outcome of making a poor decision from letting someone pressure you into something wrong?

_____
_____
_____
_____
_____
_____
_____

(True or false) Its okay if I let my sibling's pressure me beside they're family.

Wrap It Up

In a group put together a skit of showing strong confidence in peer pressure. Every group member should participate. Have fun!

Diversity

The quality or state of being different. Forms of diversity include race and listening to others ideas and views not the same as yours.

Every individual in the world are different in a unique way. Including diversity in our everyday lives consist of respecting someones race, ethnicity, age, beliefs or physical disabilities. Diversity is a way that we connect with others with humility.

Brain Power

Describe two ways that you can include diversity into your everyday life.

_____
_____
_____
_____
_____
_____

Sometimes we may not agree with different perspectives others may have. Name a time where you didn't agree but you respected what they had to say.

_____

_____

_____

_____

_____

_____

Diversity makes everyone feel accepted in society. Diversity connects all and adds value to who we are as a nation. Incorporating diversity in our lives show that we don't look at anything else besides that we are the same as humans and we matter to each other.

Describe a time you were treated differently because of your age, race, or opinion.

_____

_____

_____

_____

_____

_____

(True or false) It's okay for me to not invite the boy that's in a wheel chair at school to my party because he is different. Everyone will say I had a boring party.

Wrap It Up

In a group we will take the diversity pledge to sign it and recite it to one another.

Test Anxiety

Test anxiety- Is a combination of tension and awkward symptoms along with worry and dread. Fear of failure usually happens before or during testing.

There are easy tips to test taking observe the list below.

- Manage your time,
- Organize material needed to be studied and learned.
- Do not test on an empty stomach; bring a lite snack with you to eat while testing.
- If you do not know an answer come back to it do not get frustrated.
- Make sure you use the restroom before testing.

Brain Power

How do you feel before you take a test do you usually feel you will pass or fail? Explain.

_____

_____

_____

_____

_____

_____

Pick two study tips from above. You will use these two to help you get focused to avoid test anxiety.

_____

_____

_____

_____

_____

_____

Take a different approach with test taking. What if we begin to take our test feeling we will pass? How we prepare usually determines what will happen during the process. If we study and gain test taking tips provided above, we can start to get excited about passing. Just believe you can and you will! You are smart, and now ready to take on a test free of anxiety.

Describe one test taking tip that you would like to share that helps you prepare.

_____

_____

_____

_____

_____

(True or False) Taking test is not a major part of your grade so, you should not care if you pass or not.

Wrap It Up

In a group create a skit preparing for a test using two tips from above to help you. Every group member is expected to participate. Have fun!

<u>Integrity</u>

The quality of being honest and having good character.

Displaying integrity is being honest when no one is watching. When we strive to be people of integrity it last for a life time. Even though integrity is mostly recognized when no ones looking. It can be recognized by teacher, peers and others around you. Having integrity builds a sense of trust in society. People will know that the things you do are fare and just.

Brain Power

Does it really matter if we show integrity or not? Explain

_____

_____

_____

_____

_____

_____

How can we show integrity in society? Explain

_____

_____

_____

_____

_____

_____

There are many ways we can show integrity in our home, community, and school. It may be simple things like seeing someone drop some money and they didn't see it, but you did. It's always situations like this that gives us a choice. The choice is up to you in the moment besides no will see you if you take the money. You will just have to deal with yourself about it. Showing integrity leads to trusting yourself!

Describe a time when you showed integrity and it was hard. Explain.

_____

_____

_____

_____

_____

_____

_____

(True or False) Showing integrity never really means anything its just so people will notice you.

Wrap It Up

In your group you will take the Integrity pledge and recite it to one another. Have fun!

Self- Esteem

Self-esteem- Confidence in one's own worth or abilities and self respect.

Self-esteem traits

- Confidence
- Respect for yourself
- Pride
- Staying well groomed
- Practicing good hygiene
- Standing up for your self

Brain Power

Describe two other self-esteem traits to add to the list.

_____

_____

_____

_____

_____

_____

Why do we need to have self-esteem?

_____

_____

_____

_____

_____

_____

Self-esteem has a lot to do with how we view and treat ourselves. There is many times where people will do things to challenge your self esteem. If you were in a school setting and you wear your hair in a style that you like, but someone tells you they don't like it. That's when self –esteem says", but I love my hair!" I like it this way! Standing up for yourself and knowing that you matter. It's ok to listen to others that have opinions but it's not ok to do everything they like. When this happens you lose your self-esteem and who you are.

What can happen to our lives when we don't have self-esteem?

_____

_____

_____

_____

_____

_____

_____

_____

(True or False) It displays good self-esteem if someone doesn't Like the way you dress, but you continue to wear the clothes you like every day.

Wrap It UP

In a group draw a picture of yourself with what you have on right now. Share your drawing with your peers. Everyone should participate even if you're not the best artist. You're a great artist to us in Girlz Inc. Have fun!

Character

Character-The mental and moral qualities distinctive to an individual.

Character traits

- Good manors
- Showing empathy
- Gratitude
- Hospitable
- Dependability
- Determination
- Creativity
- Generosity
- Kindness

Brain power

Describe two other character traits not listed above.

_____

_____

_____

_____

_____

_____

What are two negative character traits to have?

_____

_____

_____

_____

_____

_____

_____

Character says a lot about who we are. It will take some practice to get to where we need to be. When people think about us, we want to think positively about who we are. Displaying good or bad character can determine if people like to be around us as well. If you're mean and aggressive, others may avoid you. If your kind you will attract more people to want to be around you. The decision is yours. Choose kindness today!

Choose two character traits above that you would like to see yourself have. Explain why?

_____
_____
_____
_____
_____
_____
_____

(True or False) It is displaying good character to help an elderly person cross the street.

Wrap It Up

In a group take the character pledge and recite it to one another. Talk about which character traits you desire to have.

Reliability

Reliability- Capable of being relied on or dependable.

Reliability Traits:

- Calling parents and telling them where you are.
- Going to places where you said you were going and not detouring.
- Showing up for class on time.
- Staying committed to activities or sports.

Brain Power

Describe two other ways to be reliable.

_____

_____

_____

_____

_____

When people can't rely on us what can be some of the consequences?

_____
_____
_____
_____
_____
_____
_____

We show reliability in our everyday lives. When we show others they can depend on us, it builds trust. Reliability helps you to stick with commitments that you make. It feels good when people can say,"oh I know you'll be here".

(True or False) Showing up for class 2 minutes after the bell, or when class starts is showing reliability, I'm only late 2 minutes max. It doesn't matter as long as I show up.

Wrap It Up

In a group see how many words you can make out of every letter in the word reliability. Ex: Respectable.The group who has the most words wins a prize! Have fun!

Punctuality

Punctuality-Being on time or keeping appointments and scheduled engagements.

When we make punctuality to priority people know and trust that we are committed. Punctuality is key to playing a major part in our character. Others feel that you are reliable and will be present, prompt& ready to go.

Brain Power

How can being punctual affect us in school?

_____

_____

_____

_____

_____

_____

What message do we send out to others when we arrive late all the time?

_____

_____

_____

_____

_____

_____

_____

Listed below are some places to show punctuality.

School
Home
Class
Events
Job Interviews

What can be some negative responses to arriving late all the time to a job or place of importance?

_____

_____

_____

_____

_____

_____

(True or False) Being prompt shows others that you value your time and others.

Wrap It up

In a group unscramble the mystery sentence.

Lswaya whos pu no mite! Ouy vnere nokw hws'o atwcihng. Every group member should participate. Be the first to solve the scramble and receive a prize.

Accountability

Accountability- The fact or condition of being responsible.

Character traits of accountability:

- Turning in homework assignments
- Finishing chores
- Keeping commitments
- Accepting responsibility for your actions

Brain power

Describe two other ways to show accountability.

_____

_____

_____

_____

_____

If we do not display accountability in our lives will people trust us? Explain?

_____

_____

_____

_____

_____

_____

_____

_____

Accountability is a way to show that you are trustworthy and responsible to a certain thing or task. In society we are known by or actions. Be someone that others know that they can count on you. It's your name and face that comes to remembrance. Be accountable at all times.

What can be some great benefits of being accountable?

_____

_____

_____

_____

_____

_____

_____

(True or false) Accountability will take you far in your career.

Wrap It Up

In a group create a positive word for each letter in **accountability**. Each group member is required to participate. Ex: A-Amazing. Have Fun!

Self Control

Self control- The ability to control oneself in emotions or desires. Displaying discipline in behavior.

Character traits of self control:

- No shouting out
- Walking away from confrontations
- Waiting on your turn to speak (not blurting out)
- Non- Violent
- Respecting others space

Brain Power

Describe two other ways to practice self control.

_____
_____
_____
_____
_____
_____

Does having self control help you or the other person? Explain.

_____

_____

_____

_____

_____

_____

Having self control is not always easy; People will do and say things that we don't like. Practicing self control always helps us to build patience and discipline. Learning when to speak and how to do it appropriately matters to every situation that we encounter.

Can there be negative consequences for not practicing self control?

_____

_____

_____

_____

_____

_____

(True or false) People should say what they want to say, and how they want to say it.

Wrap It Up

In group put together a short skit displaying good self control every group member should participate. Have fun.

Respect

Respect- A feeling of deep admiration for someone or something. Reverence, esteem, or regards.

Character traits of respect:

- Giving your seat for an elderly person
- Obeying your parents
- Not talking back
- Raising hands in class to be called on

Brain Power

Describe two other ways to show respect.

_____

_____

_____

_____

_____

_____

What is dis-respect?

_____

_____

_____

_____

_____

_____

Showing respect is one of the things we do to show we care. There are times when we may feel someone may not deserve our respect but it is never o.k to be dis-respectful. We have been taught to show respect only when it's given, that is completely not true. We have to be the bigger individual and show a big character trait of maturity and assurance to do what is right.

How can showing a person respect help you in society?

_____

_____

_____

_____

_____

_____

(True or False) If you show respect you will always get it in return.

Wrap It Up

In a group take the respect pledge. Recite it to one another. Have fun!

Dedication

Dedication- The quality of being committed to a task.

It shows good character to commit ourselves to a task or situation. When we display that we are trustworthy and dependable people know they can count on us. It helps us in our careers to be dedicated to what we do. Employers always observe timely people that are always in place.

Brain Power

In what ways can we show dedication to someone or something?

_____

_____

_____

_____

_____

_____

When we show dedication to something or someone does it help you are them?

_____

_____

_____

_____

_____

_____

Dedication can help us in so many ways. When we are not dedicated it hurts us and show people that we do not care and respect what we are doing.

What are some things that can happen negatively if we don't show dedication to important things?

_____

_____

_____

_____

_____

_____

(True or False) Dedication is not that important in this life.

Wrap It Up

Make a list of some of the things you would like to show dedication to. You may share with one other person. Have fun!

Courage

Courage-The quality of mind that enables a person to face difficulty without fear. Being brave.

Courage is what we need to face troubles or situations without fear. It is not easy to have courage. To have it you must conquer being afraid. There are many things that make us feel scared, or unable to approach something. Courage will see us through.

Brain power

Describe a time you felt afraid to do something.

_____

_____

_____

_____

_____

_____

Describe a time you used courage instead of being afraid.

_____

_____

_____

_____

_____

_____

Ways to show courage:

- Courage to tell the truth
- Courage to speak up
- Courage to dream
- Courage to say no
- Courage to stand up

How can we show courage in society?

_____

_____

_____

_____

_____

_____

(True or False) Displaying courage is just another way to be brave.

Wrap It Up

In a group exchange one way to display courage with your group members. Every member is expected to participate. Have fun!

Compassion

Compassion-Sympathetic Pity and concern for the sufferings or misfortunes of others.

Compassion is showing someone that you care about their situation. Displaying compassion is another way to express humility. Every person in a displaced circumstance will know your heart and can be re positioned in their life from the compassion that you give.

Brain power

What are two ways to show compassion in our everyday lives?

_____

_____

_____

_____

_____

_____

_____

Describe a time where you showed someone compassion.

_____

_____

_____

_____

_____

_____

_____

Many times in society we encounter a lot of situations where we see homelessness and displacement. It is up to us to have compassion and understand what people go through. Another way we can show compassion is to say to someone,"I'm sorry this has happened to you".

Does compassion always have to be shown through giving money?

_____

_____

_____

_____

_____

_____

_____

(True or False) Compassion should not be shown if people have a lot of money.

Wrap It Up

In a group put a skit together showing compassion to someone. Every group member is expected to participate. Have fun!

Writing Paper

Writing Paper

Writing Paper

Writing Paper

Writing Paper

Writing Paper

Writing Paper

Writing Paper

Writing Paper

Writing Paper

Writing Paper

Writing Paper

Writing Paper

Writing Paper

Writing Paper

Writing Paper

Writing Paper

Writing Paper

Writing Paper

Writing Paper

Writing Paper

Writing Paper

Writing Paper

Writing Paper

Writing Paper

Writing Paper

Writing Paper

Doodle Pad

Doodle Pad

Doodle Pad

Doodle Pad

Doodle Pad

Doodle Pad

Doodle Pad

Doodle Pad

Doodle Pad

Doodle Pad

Doodle Pad

www.ingramcontent.com/pod-product-compliance
Lightning Source LLC
Chambersburg PA
CBHW052003280526
45793CB00005B/840